I0750280

FINISHING LINE PRESS
www.finishinglinepress.com

Diving and Rising

poems by

Lois Rosen

Finishing Line Press
Georgetown, Kentucky

Diving and Rising

ISBN 978-1-64662-435-5 First Edition

ACKNOWLEDGMENTS

"At the Conservatory Orchid Show" and "Fire Hydrant Hero" forthcoming in *Evening Street Review.*
"Autumn Garden," "Beforehand," and "But They Look So Cute" in *Arlijo* (Arlington Literary Journal).
"In the Thorn Bushes" in *New Verse News*, based on "One of the Deadliest Places on the Southwest Border," the *NY Times,* April 18, 2019, written by Manny Fernandez and Nubia Reyna.
"Lynne's Gold," in *Peregrine Journal.*
"My Parents Used to Say" in *Calyx.*
"Not a Professional Ballerina" in *VoiceCatcher, She Holds the Face of the World,* and *Where We've Been.*
"The Students Walk Out Anyway" in *New Verse News* and *Terra Incognita.*
"Yelapa Regret" in *Verseweavers.*

With heartfelt thanks to the Peregrine Poets: Eleanor Berry, Stephanie Lenox, Ada Molinoff, Steve Slemenda, Paul Suter, Penina Ava Taesali, Colette Tennant, Dina Triest, and Marilyn Johnston. And a joyful thank you to the Trillium Writers, the ICL Writing Group, PDX Writers, Prosebuds, The Community of Writers, Centrum, Women's Group, all my marvelous teachers, editors, precious friends, and family who have encouraged and supported me including David, Bree, Slavey, Meredith, and most especially, Kevin.

Publisher: Leah Huete de Maines
Editor: Christen Kincaid
Cover Art: Deanna White
Author Photo: Richard Berry
Cover Design: Elizabeth Maines McCleavy

Printed in the USA on acid-free paper.
Order online: www.finishinglinepress.com
also available on amazon.com

Author inquiries and mail orders:
Finishing Line Press
P. O. Box 1626
Georgetown, Kentucky 40324
U. S. A.

Table of Contents

WATER BORN

Mom insists my old swim cap has *plenty*
of wear left, though yellowed,
and the strap pinches. But I'm tucking
my hair into a new one, dotted with stars,
I paid for myself.

She and her friends wear fru fru caps
topped with rubber roses. They dawdle
at the pool's edge, finally stand minutes
in the shallow end to cool off
taking dips just to their armpits.

Don't hit your head when you dive,
Mom says. Give me a break. I know
what I'm doing. Turning from her, I
snug the cap over my ears. After years
of lessons, I speed across hot concrete.

At the deep end, freed from yammering
mothers, I curl my toes over the pool's edge.
No springboard, my muscles loft me
beyond sticky Yonkers humidity, my head
centered in the arrow of my straight arms.

Water caresses my skin, closer fitting
than any bathing suit. Immersed, surfacing
only for air. Gravity cannot tame me.
Pool walls don't stop my somersaults.
I'm a spinner dolphin—diving and rising.

CAMP SHAMPOO

I swirl the tingly water of Lake Tiorati.
New York nights cool under stars. This
upstate camp is not terrifying. Never in my
summer life do Jewish girls wear yellow
cloth stars on blouses above our breasts.

A pearl of Prell drops slowly into green gel,
thick as honey, and rises in silk waves.
No rocks or broken shells cut our soles.
We reach onto the dock for Palmolive
ovals that nestle in the palms of our hands.

With the fragrant soap made of palm oil
from the Holy Land, olives from ancient
trees, we take turns soaping each other's
backs, laughing, anointing ourselves
goddesses. I hold my soap posed

like the Statue of Liberty, Grandma's
first view of America. Next summer, will
I write letters home from camp or receive
ones saying, *Wish you were here?*
My family says, *You never know.*

FIRE HYDRANT HERO

Yonkers is a desert with no oases, no camels transporting us
like sultans. Who cares? We have Louie Rutgers, who never
orders us kids, even once, to call him Louis or Mr. Rutgers.

Louie knows I'm Lois Liebowitz, and the girl in apartment
1-H is Susie O'Conner, and that the D'Apices live on the fifth floor,
all of us *baby boomer* kids, not that we know what that means.

What we do know is that our Louie hefts a wrench, long as our
arms, and as superintendent fixes the broken things in our 96
family building, yet his beefy hands do not punch or spank.

Maybe quadruple the size of mine, his hands take his wrench
and screw it to the lid on the fire hydrant, smack in front of
our building, Singer Arms.

He doesn't curse, but pulls so hard his shirt's stinky
with sweat. If each one of us little kids tried, even
all at the same time, we couldn't budge the bolt.

We know a fireman's supposed to open a hydrant, but Louie
unscrews the top. Eek, eek, sputter, pow wow! A geyser erupts.
We kids drench ourselves in icy glitter. Take that, mean sun.

We rush in, wiggle, leap, twirl—girl and boy pinwheels, flying
fish, sprites. When the festival finishes, clothes drip. Hair streams.
We shout, *Three cheers for Louie the Super! The Super! The Super!*

MRS. COOPER, 1958

(after Kim Stafford)

No other teacher I knew dyed her hair green
on St. Patrick's Day, while we sat, hands folded
on desks, inkwells unused since we with-it, slick
fifth graders wrote our cursive with ballpoints.

We tried on grass skirts, leis, necklaces of shells
from her travels to the gleaming beaches of Oahu.
She played a record of Hawaiian ukulele music,
while we swayed, hula-ing down the desk rows.

Ocean surf whispered in our ears from conches. Our
hands cupped a coconut she guided us to crack, drink
the water, eat the pulp. Using her map, we celebrated
discovering our soon-to-be-50th state was all islands.

She read Greek and Roman myths to us because they
were ancient and famous, and we fifth graders deserved
to know what-was-what about Athena defeating Poseidon,
Pandora and her perilous box, Atlas, shouldering the world.

She took us to Manhattan and gave us each Strathmore
drawing paper. Inside the Museum of Modern Art, she freed
us to find a painting, photograph, or sculpture we liked, take
a good half hour to sketch, and write why we selected it.

She trusted us to go anywhere in the museum, just be back
in the lobby at 2:00 p.m. to return to blah Yonkers. Though
we lived outside the Big Apple, that school year, we stretched
our mouths wide and relished every juicy bite.

GARDEN CONVERSATION

Light splashed this morning
on the shell-pink anemones
swaying on their tall stems
—Stanley Kunitz

Japanese Anemones survive in my yard
with haphazard care. Mom's remembered
voice jabs, *You think you know everything.*
Darn it, she was right. I don't.

But I do recognize Japanese Anemones,
their thin stems holding up six pink flowers.
Arching, the plants look like ballerinas,
limber and strong.

Anemones, also called Windflowers,
seem unbreakable, but when I arrange
shafts to show them off, some stems
break off in my hands.

The *Sunset Garden Guide* suggests staking,
explains their pink "petals" are sepals
or bracts, The species began in China, not
Japan. Mom would say, *Who knew?* I didn't.

Mom's only flowers were a table decoration
she won at a luncheon, Mother's Day orchids.
Her sweet potato in a glass had vines reaching
toward our kitchen window.

Mom never had a garden. I bow toward
Anemones' pale, green pea-size centers.
Minuscule fringes quiver around them.
I stroke the velvety stems.

HIS RECLINER

Dad's recliner, the bushed, workingman's throne,
its faded aqua fabric worn around the armrests,
the headrest, greasy with Brylcreem, blended
odors with sweat, his office-shirt's laundry-starch,
and whiffs of each morning's rusty-smelling styptic
pencil dabbed on razor nicks to staunch the blood.

I could only guess how the cuts stung his left cheek,
already red from radiation. No matter how ragged
the recliner, given his suffering, first from childhood
polio, then malignant jaw cancer, thank God, in remission,
Mom wouldn't fight him to buy a new recliner, since
he swore the old one fit his body perfectly.

Who'd begrudge his need to locate it in the living room
corner beside the window fan in beastly summers, years
before air conditioning? Frigid winters, cellar boilers shot
steam-heat into our radiator. Alive, earning good wages,
each workday he headed out, driving all over the Bronx,
Westchester, and upstate to Rockland County,

doing Department of Labor Wage and Hour Investigations,
foregoing lunch, home late afternoons, drinking only water
all day because of his jaw condition. No matter how many
times he said, resting in his recliner, *You'll be well-provided*
for, head back, feet up. *Be nice to me. I might die soon.*
Wasn't he joking? He had to be. I rarely considered where

his savings from not purchasing a new recliner or items
he denied himself were going. He often leaned back
and played his favorite record of Frank Sinatra crooning
I'll Be Seeing You. We sang the ending together, *I'll be*
looking at the moon, but I'll be seeing you. Too soon
silence shrouded the living room and the empty recliner.

THE PATH OF TOTALITY

What I learned to love about the eclipse
was the egalitarianism—the moon and sun
belonging to everyone, lucky to watch,
no immigration ban on viewing the sky.

I'd mowed our lawn, but didn't weed—
as the moon described its arc, aligning
itself that morning across the sun, total
daylight-darkness above my home.

Reverse-image patterns scalloped paths,
while the corona's halo embraced
the black moon, and I burst out singing
The Best Things in Life Are Free.

YOU LOOK FACHALISHT

Here, taste my chicken soup.
Did you ever see such golden fat?

What will it hurt? Go ahead
Treat yourself to a shtikeleh rye bread

Some nice schmaltz
Just a shmear.

And my matzo balls
Delicious, no?

Made with my own two hands
Over the hot stove

But for you, darling
It was worth it.

Here, Bubela, at least
Try these gribenes,

Onion in chicken fat,
So what, it smears your hands.

Take. Take.
You call that a portion?

You, who don't know
What real fachalisht is.

My parents used to say,

you have a big mouth, but when I taught
in the South Bronx, landlords burned
buildings to get insurance money, doors
of my middle-school students' apartments
quadruple-locked, discarded needles dotted
streets, the Model Cities Program left lots
full of rubble from buildings torn down,
none rebuilt, and my car had a steering
wheel lock, hood lock, gas tank lock,
locking hubcaps, all this true, I got up at
five a.m. to type the daily magazine
featuring their stories and named it *Big*
Mouth, and we sat in a circle each morning,
reading their writing aloud, while my mom
complained, *You're out of your mind,*
because I was taking a classroom of kids
on the subway to Coney Island Beach,
the Metropolitan Opera's free kid concerts,
the Natural History Museum, including
one afternoon trip to an avian specialist's
office in Manhattan because students
found a duck with a rope embedded
in its torn, scabbed leg, body slanting
away from the direction, we guessed
it had been tied, and kids from the projects,
despite my mom saying, *You go in there,*
you're taking your life in your hands,
collected change, we rushed to a ritziest
of the rich block on Park Ave., where
the bird vet removed the rope, stitched up
the sedated duck's leg, applied salve,
gauze, and told us the handful of coins
was plenty, after which, a kiddie pool
appeared in our classroom, students took
turns treating the wounds, and the duck
opened its bill quacking, no one telling her
to shut her big mouth, and besides, as far
as we knew, by the end of the school year,
the duck was driven to Westchester for
a luxury life in a pond, my mother said,

You did what for a fakakta duck? but that's
if I told her or my father about the duck
because they warned me many many times,
It's better not to be too honest, and
Sometimes you have to lie, so who's to say?

NO PICNIC

My birthday is the same day my mother died, forty-six years after I was born. I'm not making this up. She used to say, "Did you forget you had a mother?" when she called me in Oregon from New York. I was not a good daughter, who phoned regularly or sent frequent letters. I was the escape artist, the magician's disappearing woman, who didn't vanish, but fled as far across the country as I could, calling her because I forced myself to, inviting her to visit once a year only, making myself go see her each summer for a dreaded week of boredom. If only she had a daughter who shared her interests. I hated how we'd lived in that tiny, no privacy, one-bedroom apartment, with her and Dad sleeping on the convertible sofa and me in the bedroom, all sharing the closet and bureau drawers, a room like Grand Central Station with them huffing in and out to get what they needed. She smoked like a non-stop locomotive stinking up the air. No wonder I kept getting bronchitis. She wasn't all bad. Not really. She paid for me to have opportunities she didn't have like dance classes, summer camp, violin lessons. She cooked, bought me clothes. If only she hadn't believed the way you raise a daughter is to criticize, rarely praise, her words an acrid smoke. I was the miracle baby. I was not supposed to have a swelled head or a big mouth. Dad had jaw cancer before I was born, and after radiation, she never got to travel with him, nor could they eat out. Her life was no picnic. I didn't say it out loud, but I blamed her for his death. I was already married and not living with my parents then. She waited to call an ambulance till the morning. Would he have survived if she'd called sooner? I shared little of my adult life with her, so why does her mink coat still hang in my closet in Oregon twenty-four years after she died? I've tried it on but never worn fur in public, embarrassed to appear in animal skins. It seems so gruesome. How happy she was to have money to finally purchase the swanky coat for herself after dad died. Why didn't *I* buy her extravagant gifts, too, give her something lavish she'd get pleasure from? About my birthday, I still don't understand how her body could have chosen that particular day to die. Was it to make sure I'd remember her? Was it a rebuke, revenge, a way to cast a pall on my celebrations? Did cellular memory recall when significant events happened in her life? I do have in my closet one hanger covered with her crocheting. It holds clothes well. When she was making many as presents, I thought how deadly dull. Today, I wish I had more.

RECLINERS AND BLACKBERRIES

My grown son, who hasn't lived here since college, chides me
for having the living-room recliner reupholstered and moved
to my office. He eyes me with a *Mom-how-could-you look.*

But there's a new ochre recliner exactly where the old one
always was. He says, *It's not comfortable.* Too quickly I answer,
It feels fine to me. The old one was torn. But I understand.

In the old recliner, he sat on my lap while we read *Goodnight Moon,*
Harry the Dirty Dog, Do You Know How Much I Love You?
Older, he took pride of place in that chair, reading, drawing
his dad, himself, and me together. No replacement needed.

~

At nine, he cried the week before I remarried. My father-in-law-
to-be mowed our tangled yard with his huge tractor, transforming
the overgrown mess into a park. My son sobbed, *He killed*
my favorite blackberry bush. But there are more, I said.

Blackberries regrow fast. Just look. They're all over. He would
not face where I pointed. I wish I'd hugged him, said, *I'm really*
sorry. I know you loved that bush. It's sad to lose a thing you love.

He wept. *It was my favorite one.* At least, I knew better than to
scare my little one by warning: They have sharp thorns.
Watch out. Cuts hurt. Even the sweetest berries leave stains.

THE PROGNOSIS

It's just basal cell, the least
invasive carcinoma,
the best. The biopsy incision
probably took it all from
my face. To confirm no spread
my dermatologist rechecks
margins. She's reassured.
The prognosis is good.

Daddy's cancer never spread.
Despite the tubes, disfiguring
surgery, radiation-burned cheek,
seventy-pound weight-drop.
The hospital psychiatrist
asked about suicidal thoughts,
but Daddy insisted, *I want*
a child to live for—

Me. I'm fortunate. After all,
the spot's so easy to hide
under my bangs. And seared
nose dots dry fast to scabs.
I've no reason for complaint
like he had losing his good
looks after a carved-out cheek.

I expected cancer would cut
his life short. I was wrong.
At fifty-three, he died of
undetected diabetes. Forty-eight
years later, I still hear him call me,
Shaina madela, beautiful girl,
a living doll.

Now, I, of course, insist
on blood-sugar tests. So far
none have shown up positive.
Lucky me.

POETRY IN ESL CLASS

Working past midnight,
Javier gets up at five a.m.
to bake empanadas
for our class. He considers
a teacher, an opal,
shining in the darkness.

Pilar floats into the classroom,
her hair loose to the middle
of her back. She writes
I am colibri, the hummingbird,
radiant feathers, vibrating wings.

Evelina tells our class
she admires poets,
looking at
each little stone,
each star.

WHY THE PHONE RANG SO EARLY

By the Santiam
June evening
After work
Beer and burritos
Breezes
River smells
Angel and Miguel
Laughing

White teenagers
Drunk
Go back to Mexico
Grapefruit size rocks
Angel and Miguel
Try to drive away
Later an ambulance
Police call

June morning
Raquel waits
Weeping
At our classroom door
Teacher
You hear
What happened
I nod slowly

Hector
Asks
You listen to the news
My book bag drops
I carry your books
You hand me keys
I will open

Raquel and Hector
Here
Twenty-six more
Here

Angel

Absent

Miguel

Absent

IN THE THORN BUSHES

Migrants have been dying in the South Texas brush.
Many, many are dying. That was what surprised me.
The President insists he's shocked. But now that he
knows for sure, do you see him rushing from a private
dinner to order humanitarian convoys of food and water?
Eight bodies were found this year, and it's only mid-April.
Among the cactus, mesquite, sage, oak, thorn bushes,
the lost, frozen, dazed, sick men and women collapse
from heatstroke, hypothermia, dehydration. A sheriff
today found a female skeleton face down, in dirt,
U.S., Mexican, and Honduran cash around her, prayer
cards in the pockets of her jeans. A male body, face up,
a Honduran I.D. in his wallet, he's discovered to be
the father of a three-year-old girl. There's a selfie of
the two of them on his Facebook page. In Spanish, he
called her *my princess*. The sheriff runs out of body bags.
How does someone get used to bagging up the dead?

THE STUDENTS WALK OUT ANYWAY

Although a Needville, Texas principal
threatens suspension,

though parents in Billings, Montana warn
they'll ground their kids,

though the NRA tweets an AR15 photo
I'll control my own guns, thank you,

though South Carolina Governor McMaster
calls the walkout *left wing* and *shameful,*

though the church shooter's sister hisses
I hope it's a trap and they all get shot,

students join hands, make speeches,
chant, read victims' names,

hold signs, sob, pray, stand silent
for six minutes. There are no words.

LYNNE'S GOLD

I found the gold ring in my late
sister-in-law's jewelry box
slipped it on my finger
and wore the band daily
until it broke.

Gold, I believed, remained strong.
We say *solid gold.* But I learned
from a jeweler—gold is so soft
it's common that rings
bend or crack.

My solid sister-in-law cut down
our Christmas tree, shimmied
up oaks to shake mistletoe loose,
taught decades of middle-schoolers,
fostered one of her students.

After retirement, she led Relay
for Life teams, hauled immense
garbage bags full of pop cans
from doctors' clinics, donated
redemptions to the Cancer Society.

This week, the jeweler restored
her flattened ring to its full circle.
After a polishing, the gold glows.
If only the oncologists had found
a potion to restore her health.

Lynne, oh, Lynne,
I miss your ringing laughter,
your fourteen-karat kindness.

MERMAID GIFT

This year, she doesn't accompany me to her Bronx
building's luxurious pool because exercise hurts
her back, but my friend bought a book of passes
for me to enjoy swimming without her.

Swishing in the silky water, cushioned on a chaise,
I think of Hans Christian Anderson's tale, how
the invisible mermaid floats in air, envying girls
for three hundred years, becoming human only
when the children behave.

I eye the clock, not wanting to be gone long,
head to her apartment cocooned
to my ankles in her terrycloth robe.

She lived in Denmark during Nazi occupation.
In that dark tale, did she feel invisible waiting
for release?

She sends me her Royal Copenhagen mermaid
in bubble wrap, the bronze statue in the harbor
fused to rock. Her gift emerges intact from
the UPS box. The harbor statue was defaced,
decapitated, stolen by hoodlums, repaired.

In my home, she's naked porcelain,
visible through breakfront glass.

AT THE CONSERVATORY ORCHID SHOW

Still statuesque at eighty-nine, she powers
toward six-thousand-plus cascading flowers
doesn't complain of back pain. Bless her,
widowed twice, a retired Bronx teacher

of special education, she's come to savor
Oncidium Splendidum's shades of lavender,
the yellow Goldianas and Lady Slippers
blossoming pale pink to dark, sultry colors.

Despite the crowd and fierce New York winter,
she positions herself under the rainbow, closer
to the forty-five million-year-old species, admires
the blossoms lying on the stone floor,

bends to gently lift a few—fallen, rare—
to live their last days at home in her care.

AUTUMN GARDEN

As the older woman yanks
a stake from the perennial border
her legs slip sideways like
Carol Burnett's in a pratfall
but this is no comedy.

Slamming the driveway
she hears her hip crack.
Independent fool. Hadn't
her daughter begged her to
wear an emergency clicker?

Why buy a befuddling cell
contraption, when she pays
good money for a landline?
She tries to inch to the porch,
but pain sears.

Not one to blubber. What she
wouldn't give for a strong cup
of coffee. Gravel stabs her ankle.
She catches whiffs of smoke
from leaf-burning.

The spade remains upright.
How long has she been dozing?
The last asters flutter like her
once-upon-a-time prom dress.

BEFOREHAND

6:00 a.m. pre-op
in a curtained-off room
overhead lights glare

My friend hands me
her Advance Directive
whom to contact in case

Gripping the lists I hope
to notify those named
of a successful surgery

The kidney removal
will be laparoscopic
No surprises please

At least the problem
is congenital not cancer
and there's a second kidney

A nurse tells her to undress
put on the paper gown
climb onto the bed now

Everything she wore
from home must go
into the clear plastic bag

The fanny pack with her wallet
cellphone and keys she must
hand me for safekeeping

Used to living by herself
will she feel my watching
listening notetaking intrusive

but she says *Sit here close*
grasps my hand welcomes
me to this intimacy

her hand delicate   mine
meatier   our fingers twined
Icy palms warm together

FAULTY MECHANISMS

My friend confirmed with the hospital.
All rooms have recliners. Yes, someone
can stay with you. Perfect, I'll be at
the patient's side. But not so fast.

Waking 3:20 a.m., at Admitting by 5:30,
later pacing, fretting, checking a screen
10:12 A.M., I'm told the surgery went well.
It's what matters. Wonderful news. Still

my friend's rolled into a tiny-windowed,
prison-cell-sized room. No recliner.
Where would one fit? My best guess
—nowhere.

Nor will my five-foot-three body manage
to lie down on a two-foot wide, three-foot-
long, thin-cushioned window-seat.
Not a chance.

I will not abandon my friend for a motel,
but I refuse to lie on the hospital floor
with the germs. Haven't complained
yet,

don't need to because my friend wakes
near noon, requests anti-nausea meds,
looks around, despite dizziness, asks
the nurse, *Where's the recliner?*

Two hours pass. An aide rolls in a massive
recliner, sized for a grizzly bear.
Room door partially blocked, no easy
exit. How can this be legal?

When a bouquet of sunflowers, lilies, and roses
flashes color through the door's gap, a delivery
man's arm thrusts the vase inside the room—
family wishes, floral fragrances.

Nurses wedge through, must have noticed.
My pale friend, this very day of surgery, woken
in her bed again, gets rolled on an elevator up
to a large room with a recliner. Relief.

Except raising the footrest, lowering the back
takes a Hercules. I have to hurl myself against
the chair-back. Will I end up a patient?
Rods scream like a heavy-metal band.

My friend should sleep. If I were a gymnast
I could leap over the armrests. The demon
chair shrieks whenever I get in or out,
but I will rise whenever she needs water.

Party

Midnight after surgery,
inflated cuffs pump air
around my friend's ankles.
A catheter confines her
to a hospital bed. Awake,
I'm a few meters away in
a recliner. A nurse enters,
takes vitals and mentions
snacks in a freezer. The
patient asks for a cherry
popsicle. It has two sticks.
Once the nurse leaves, I
break the treat in two, half
for each of us. Shh! Don't
tell staff the dear patient
waves me to climb up,
perch on the bed's edge.
Partners in crime—she,
in a sans-fashion gown,
me, in my new-surely-germ
-free, Penney's, year-end,
baggy fleece. We loft
pop halves like two
queens signaling
by mutual
accord, May
the festivities
commence.

Licking icy sweetness,
we agree the popsicle,
tasting like cough syrup,
might contain a healing
potion. The color, watered-
down, compared with
cherries, provides cool,
refreshing licks, while no
staff stops our revelry for
pressure checks, blood
draws. What if ruby-tinged
drips leave traces of the
bacchanal on the blanket?
We chuckle, partners in not-
so-sterile sharing, hoping
staff won't disband jubilant
celebration. Who knew a
popsicle could generate
so much giggling? Ecstatic,
my friend is able to sit up,
to eat, even if only a popsicle.
Tongues tingle, licking drips,
we're kids again,
friends for life
at our
two-guest
hush hush
party.

A MONTH BEHIND

for A. B.

My calendar shows April
but it's already May

If I could go back, we'd be
strolling your neighborhood

blossoming white and pink
camellia lush in your yard

daffodils trumpeting yellow
tulips flashing their satin

you leaning on my arm
crossing Mill Creek Bridge

~

May's heat burns the lilac
Daffodils shrivel to husks

You ask me to buy you bright
jackets with pockets

tired of stained blouses
your notebook out of reach

Petals blown from branches
disappear in days

Your rosemary plants remain
fragrant perennials

SEVENTY IS THE NEW SIXTY. MAYBE SO,

until a knee gives way, your orthopedist
diagnoses *a frayed meniscus*, advises no
surgery yet. *Let the membrane stay*
a cushion, so bone won't rub bone.
Do physical therapy and hope, fingers
crossed. You've received a reprieve.

Seventy aims for sixty, if you want Botox,
a form of botulism shot into wrinkled lips,
after creams with age-fighting formulas
promised replenishment, younger skin
dewy in weeks, though creases deepen. Still
puckering up can mean *Let's kiss,* when
a love lasts despite the puckers of age.

Seventy is still seventy when you sit at
the computer, phone-alarm for breaks
ignored, and after four or three or two
hours your lower back stiffens, bent legs
remaining rigid at right angles like rusted
bridge-chairs needing WD 40 to unbend,
but despite arthritis, you've kept writing.

At seventy when a decade seems to have
vanished, little lines ray around your mouth
like exclamation marks of joy and pain
etched in your face, a journey mapped.
You're a person, not an age.

DANCE PRO

Of course, I want to be a pro on *Dancing with the Stars*
like Karina Smirnoff performing a romantic rumba,
her body sinuous and hot. Her teaching makes complex
routines look easy despite her mis-stepping partner,
a triple-crown-winning jockey, who rarely danced before.
Despite two 7's and one 6 tonight, with last night's scores
and the viewer votes tallied, pro and partner get cut.

We watch in the living room, my husband and I, sitting
during each dance, pressed close, his hands warming mine.
Commercial time, we break apart, do laundry, pay bills
—a benefit of regular channels though we love PBS.
We race back for the next couple. Val and Tamar perform
their jazzy Charleston while I lie on the floor draped across
a Styrofoam half rod, letting my shoulders droop, a therapy
exercise to improve posture, which the judges stress.

We return to the couch as Paula Dean, rumored racist,
drapes her bosom and thighs like a boa constrictor
around Louis, her pro from Amsterdam, a five-time world-
ballroom champ. He handles the predator with stoic
dignity. Judges warn her, *Memorize the choreography.*
Soon Louis will be free to rejoin the dance troupe, no
hope of winning the mirror ball, its squares glittering.

We're back on the couch, tapping our feet, snuggling.
Maybe this beats being a pro. I give us a 9.

DEAR GRANDDAUGHTER,

(after visiting Ellis Island)

Now that you are old enough,
your question I will answer.

There was only one thing on my mind.
when I escaped Russia. I wanted to
get out of there and come to America.

In Antwerp, Belgium:
Questions on the manifest:
Name, height, eye color,
job, money? *Are you a criminal?*
Are you an anarchist?

They fumigated and de-loused.
On board they gave us a tin plate,
cup and spoon.
Weeks passed.
We didn't see the sky.

I hate to tell you what I looked like.
One suitcase I had with me.
Clinging to family,
we could warm each other.
I'm going to a free land.
I'll never go back to Russia.
I never want to see it again.

Ellis Island, they handed us food.
I'd never seen a banana.
White bread was like cake already.

What did I have there?
Absolutely nothing.
When I came here
I was in a different world
finally, finally.

In America
there was a future.
There was hope.
There was *you*.

AMORE

I'm not saying N.Y. pizza isn't tasty,
nor denying that on the Bronx's
Arthur Ave., I breathed in real
sauce, prosciutto, fresh mozzarella.

But in Rome, maybe it's the purer wheat,
the *rosso* red of local tomatoes, water,
the guide in *Trastevere* urges us to drink
from faucets rising from cobblestones.

Maybe it's recipes passed for generations
in a bakery like *Forno*. Maybe flavors
diluted when emigrants crossed the Atlantic.
Maybe too much salt was lost in their tears.

Foot-wide slabs of garnished dough
lie side by side on a *trattoria* counter.
Sorry a semester's Italian clots in my brain,
I point to the one I want

with spicy sauce, cheeses, and roasted garlic,
gesture how much. The counter man lifts my
section into the oven. Simmering sauce romances
bubbling cheese. Burnt crust enlivens the tang.

Bite after bite, I forget raven-haired, dark-
eyed Adonises on Vespas vrooming past.
It's first-bite love, a Roman holiday
of taste buds crooning, *That's Amore,*
Amore, Amore.

YELAPA REGRET

Four-legged, seaside swain sashays
into my no-door, open-air *palapa*
along with smells of grilling tortillas
raucous *chachalaca* birdcall clatter.

Light brown, maybe a Labrador mix
more surfer dude than simpering pet
a guest without reservations, here
for a one-nighter, perhaps longer,

a stray with no collar. I back away
fretting about fleas and bites. "Shoo!
Vállate!" I wave. He trots out, no
barking or growling, dignity intact.

His name's *Canelo*, male version
of cinnamon I'm told. *Playa* dogs
are peaceful. Minutes later, he curls
up on the next-door woman's cot.

Your loss, Lady. I could've snuggled
beside you this moonlit night under
the mosquito net. Me, the local.
Qué lástima. What a shame.

NOT A PROFESSIONAL BALLERINA

I'm a kindergartener, showing off my sunset-gold, satin-topped
leotard, with the triple-layered, stiff net tutu, sticking way, way out,

wearing black leather ballerina slippers on the day-camp bus,
where Stanley, our driver grins. "You look beautiful,"

and I bow for my fans. I am the dancer who does not change
into shorts or a bathing suit all day.

~

Finally twelve, promoted to dance *en pointe*, I slip my feet
into pink satin toe shoes. Lambswool puffs caress my toes.

Long pink satin ribbons crisscross my ankles. I teeter on
tippy toes, rising *relevé, pas de bourrée,* and, *assemblée*, aloft.

In the mirrored room, at the barre, I *plié, arabesque*, let go,
float above Mrs. Berliner's live piano's Debussy, Tchaikovsky.

~

Now 71, at Jazzercise—no barre, no mirrored walls, not
one tutu, any old sneakers, ceiling fans to cool hot flashes,

I move to "Uptown Funk," "Love Yourself," "Rock
That Body," and the consolation of "One Call Away."

Stiff and creaky, still I grapevine, *plié, chassé,* as iPod
speakers blare, and walk sassy to "Baby, I'm Worth It."

GLOSSARY

ITALIAN

amore - love
forno - oven
rosso - red
Trastevere - a section of Rome on the West Bank of the Tiber River
trattoria - a neighborhood café or store with tasty takeout

SPANISH

Canelo - taken from *canela* – cinnamon
Chachalaca - a bird found in wooded areas of the far southern U.S., Mexico, Central, and South America.
Colibri – *hummingbird*
palapa - *a traditional Mexican open-air shelter, roofed with palm leaves or branches*
playa - *beach*
Qué lástima - *What a shame*
Vállate! - *Go away!*
Yelapa - a small beach town in Jalisco, Mexico

YIDDISH

bubeleh - sweetie, darling, a term of endearment
fachalisht - almost dying of hunger
fakakta - ridiculous, crappy
schmaltz - rendered chicken or goose fat
shaine madeleh - a pretty little girl
shmear - a smear or a spread, perhaps of cream cheese or butter
shtikeleh - a little piece of food, maybe bread or cheese

www.ingramcontent.com/pod-product-compliance
Lightning Source LLC
LaVergne TN
LVHW051022080826
845145LV00009B/2753

* 9 7 8 1 6 4 6 6 2 4 3 5 5 *